Rain Forest Babies

Kathy Darling
Photographs by Tara Darling

Walker and Company
New York

Thank you, Brad, Karen, and Megan Bonar for letting us photograph the baby Bengal tigers you are raising with such love and care at the Black Pine Animal Park in Albion, Indiana.

And thanks to macaw breeders Pat Galen and Philip Cacciatore for allowing us to photograph their babies.

Text copyright © 1996 by Kathy Darling
Photographs copyright © 1996 by Tara Darling

First published in the United States of America in 1996 by Walker Publishing Company, Inc.

Published simultaneously in Canada by Thomas Allen & Son Canada, Limited, Markham, Ontario

Library of Congress Cataloging-in-Publication Data
Darling, Kathy.
Rain forest babies / Kathy Darling ; photographs by Tara Darling.
p. cm.
Summary: Photographs and text describe some of the many unique young animals that live in the world's rain forests, including frogs, iguanas, macaws, orangutans, and tigers.
ISBN 0-8027-8411-9 (hardcover). – ISBN 0-8027-8412-7 (reinforced)
1. Rain forest fauna–Juvenile literature. 2. Animals–Infancy–Juvenile literature. [1. Rain forest animals. 2. Animals–Infancy.] I. Darling, Tara, ill. II. Title.
QL112.D37   1996
591.909'52–dc20   95-37738
CIP
AC

Map on page 3 and rain forest icons throughout the book by Dennis O'Brien.
Artwork on page 32 by Linda Howard and Elizabeth Sieferd.

Printed in Hong Kong
2 4 6 8 10 9 7 5 3 1

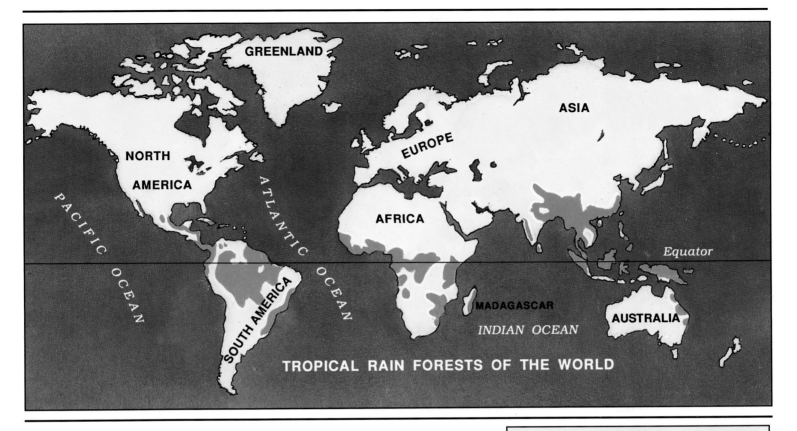

TROPICAL RAIN FORESTS OF THE WORLD

The rain forests are Earth's giant nursery. You can find new babies at any time of the year.

Half of all living things on the planet are found in the rain forests. All the tropical rain forests are alike: hot, wet, and green. But each one has animals and plants that belong to it alone.

Come and see what is hatching from the eggs and peeking out of the nests. The rain forests are home to some of the most interesting babies you will ever meet.

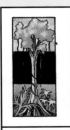

| FOREST FLOOR | UNDER-STORY | CANOPY |

These symbols appear throughout the book and represent the layer of the rain forest that each animal inhabits. For more information about these layers turn to "About the Rain Forests" on the last page of the book.

Caterpillar

The rain forest is full of bugs. They're creeping and crawling on the vines and bushes. They're flying above the treetops. Look high. Look low. Look anywhere, and you will see insects. They are there even when you can't see them. Whole armies of bugs hide under tree bark or in tunnels beneath the forest floor.

Many insect babies don't look at all like their parents. Caterpillars are young butterflies and moths.

To keep safe, these caterpillars make a little house and pull it around with them. Their mobile homes are made from a rolled-up leaf that is glued with spit. It's hard to believe these ugly wormlike creatures will become beautiful urania moths like the one above. But it happens every day in the rain forest.

Caterpillar
(Urania Moth)

❀ Birthplace: Hatches from egg laid on a bush
❀ Birth size: About 1/2 inch long
❀ Adult size: Caterpillar is 1 1/2 inches long when ready to become a moth. Wingspan of moth is 5 inches.
❀ Littermates: Hundreds, sometimes thousands
❀ Favorite food: Caterpillar eats leaves; moth drinks sweet or salty liquids.
❀ Parent care: None
❀ Enemies: Birds, frogs, insects, small mammals
❀ Home forest: Central and South America and the island of Madagascar (off the east coast of Africa)

Elephant

The biggest animal in the rain forest is the elephant. And the biggest baby is the elephant calf. Three hundred pounds at birth, it will become a thousand-pound baby in less than two years. That elephant milk is powerful stuff!

The elephant baby sucks on its trunk like a human baby sucks on its thumb. Trunks are good for other things too: sniffing, putting food and water into the mouth, and playing with sticks and leaves. This calf is part of a big family called a *herd*. There are lots of other elephant babies in the herd, but this calf is only two weeks old and still too little to play with the other babies.

Elephant
(Sumatran Elephant)

- ✿ Baby name: Calf
- ✿ Birthplace: Forest clearing
- ✿ Birth weight: 300 pounds
- ✿ Adult weight: Up to 11,000 pounds
- ✿ Littermates: None
- ✿ Favorite food: Babies drink milk; adults eat leaves and grass.
- ✿ Parent care: Baby stays with mother for 10 or more years in a herd of related females.
- ✿ Enemies: Tigers, humans
- ✿ Home forest: Sumatra (a big island in Asia)

Frog

ook, but don't touch! People who live in the rain forest know to keep away from these beautiful baby frogs. The golden froglets are small, but they are able to take care of themselves. If danger comes, a poison oozes out of their skin. This "sweat" is very deadly. The babies in the picture on the left could kill all the people on earth.

Bright gold is one of the warning colors that poison frogs use. Here are some of the bright patterns they use to say, *Danger! Keep Away.*

Frog
(Poison Arrow Frog)

- ✿ Baby name: Tadpole when young, froglet when older
- ✿ Birthplace: Hatches from egg on ground. Is carried to a pool of trapped water in the treetops by mother or father.
- ✿ Birth size: No bigger than a raisin
- ✿ Adult size: Less than 1 inch long. Can sit on a dime.
- ✿ Littermates: 2 or 3
- ✿ Favorite food: Insects, ants, tiny water animals
- ✿ Parent care: Tadpoles are fed by both parents.
- ✿ Enemies: Humans and other large animals that may step on them
- ✿ Home forest: Central and South America and the island of Madagascar

Kangaroo

Surprise! There are kangaroos in rain forests. These red-legged pademelons live on the ground. Other kinds hop around in the treetops.

All baby kangaroos have the same name. When they are carried in Mother's pouch, both boy and girl babies are called *joey*. This little one (left) is too big for the pouch, but it will keep close to its mother's side for protection. Don't let Mom's sweet face fool you. She can deliver a kick that would make a karate champion proud.

Kangaroo
(Red-legged Pademelon)

- Baby name: Joey
- Birthplace: Forest floor
- Birth weight: About the same as a grain of rice
- Adult weight: 10 pounds
- Littermates: None
- Favorite food: Babies drink milk; adults eat leaves and grass.
- Parent care: Mother carries baby in pouch. Father does not help.
- Enemies: Feral house cats, wild dogs, pythons, eagles
- Home forest: Australia

Tiger

This cute little tiger cub will grow up to be a hundred times bigger than the kitty in your house. It will do a lot of the same things a house cat does, but it will not be able to purr. The tiger is one of the "four who can roar." Three of the roaring cats—the tigers, the leopards, and the jaguars—live in rain forests. Lions, the fourth roarer, sometimes live in forests, but never in rain forests.

Tiger
(Bengal Tiger)

- ✿ Baby name: Cub
- ✿ Birthplace: Forest clearing
- ✿ Birth weight: 2 pounds
- ✿ Adult weight: Male Bengal tigers, 400 pounds; females, 250 pounds. Rain forest tigers are the smallest tigers.
- ✿ Littermates: 2 or 3
- ✿ Favorite food: Babies drink milk; adults eat meat.
- ✿ Parent care: Cubs stay with mother for 2 years. Father does not help.
- ✿ Enemies: Humans
- ✿ Home forest: India and nearby countries in Asia

Chameleon

Chameleons use skin color to send messages to each other. The "color talk" is not something they are born knowing. Like human children, they have to learn their language. Baby chameleons are born pale brown. The only color they can make is green, which helps them hide from enemies. It takes student chameleons about a year before they are able to "read" and "write" in the rainbow colors of an adult like this one (right) from the rain forest of Madagascar.

Chameleon
(Panther Chameleon)

✿ Birthplace: Most hatch from an egg buried in the dirt or leaf litter of the forest floor. Some desert chameleons are born live.

✿ Birth size: There are 128 species of chameleon. The littlest are less than 1 inch long, and the biggest are 2 inches.

✿ Adult size: The smallest species are only as big as a fingernail. Large species can be more than 3 feet long.

✿ Littermates: Up to 100

✿ Favorite food: Insects

✿ Parent care: None

✿ Enemies: Birds, snakes

✿ Home forest: Two-thirds of all species live only on Madagascar. The rest are from Africa and some surrounding areas.

UNDER-STORY

Iguana

Baby iguanas (facing page) look like ordinary lizards. Big iguanas (above) look like something from a horror movie. But things are not always what they seem.

The babies are meat-eating hunters. The grown-ups are gentle creatures that spend their days taking sunbaths and nibbling on leaves and pretty flowers in the rain forests of Central and South America.

Iguana
(Green Iguana)

✿ Birthplace: Hatches from an egg buried in sandy soil
✿ Birth size: 10 inches, including the tail
✿ Adult size: 6 feet
✿ Littermates: As many as 50
✿ Favorite food: Babies eat insects, leaves, flowers; adults eat leaves and flowers.
✿ Parent care: None
✿ Enemies: Large lizards, snakes, jaguars, and smaller, climbing cats
✿ Home forest: Central and South America

Lemur

eet the leaping lemurs. Lemurs don't swing through the trees like monkeys. They leap. Mother lemurs leap even when they are carrying their babies.

Lemurs didn't invent piggyback rides, but the babies sure like them. Little ringtailed lemurs ride like jockeys. Brown lemur babies wrap around their mother's waist like a belt. Lepilemurs sit on Mother's back even when they are both in a nest hole.

There are more than thirty kinds of lemurs; they all live on the island of Madagascar, near Africa.

Lemur
(Lepilemur, Ringtailed Lemur, Brown Lemur)

❧ Birthplace: Trees or tree nest
❧ Birth weight: Lepilemurs, 1/2 ounce; ringtailed and browns, 1 ounce
❧ Adult weight: Lepilemurs, 1 pound; ringtailed, 5 pounds; browns, 7 pounds
❧ Littermates: None
❧ Favorite food: Babies drink milk; adults eat fruit, seeds, and leaves.
❧ Parent care: Lepilemurs, ringtailed, and browns are cared for by mothers only.
❧ Enemies: Snakes, hawks, and in some places a catlike animal called a *fossa*
❧ Home forest: The island of Madagascar, near Africa

Marmoset

Pygmy marmosets are the smallest monkeys in the world. Their babies are almost always twins. The tiny mother, only four inches long, is not strong enough to carry both babies as she jumps around in the rain forest trees. She has help. Father marmoset is a very loving parent. He washes the twins, cuddles them, plays with them, carries them, and teaches them how to find food.

Marmoset
(Pygmy Marmoset)

- ✿ Birthplace: Treetop
- ✿ Birth weight: 1/2 ounce or less
- ✿ Adult weight: 4 or 5 ounces
- ✿ Littermates: 1 (marmosets are twins)
- ✿ Favorite food: Babies drink milk; adults favor tree sap and insects.
- ✿ Parent care: Father and mother both carry babies for 2 weeks.
- ✿ Enemies: Bigger monkeys, snakes, hawks, eagles, ocelots
- ✿ Home forest: South America

CANOPY

Macaw

Mother and father macaw have the most beautiful feathers in the forest. But their chicks are naked. Totally naked! Only for a few days, though. Then fluffy "baby feathers" called *down* cover their wrinkly skin. This two-week-old Hahn's macaw (right) is warm in its down coat, but it can't fly with this kind of feather. Down isn't waterproof, either, so the baby macaw won't go far from the nest hole.

At nine weeks, a blue and gold macaw baby (left) already has most of the bright, strong feathers it will need to fly away. But the fledgling is in no hurry to leave its loving parents. Young macaws stay with their family for two or three years.

Macaw
(Hahn's Macaw, Blue and Gold Macaw)

- ❀ Baby name: Chick. Called a fledgling when it can fly.
- ❀ Birthplace: Hatches from egg laid in a tree hole
- ❀ Birth weight: 1 ounce
- ❀ Adult size: Hahn's macaw, 1 foot long; blue and gold macaw, 3 feet long
- ❀ Nest mates: 2
- ❀ Favorite food: Partly digested fruit and seeds brought by parents
- ❀ Parent care: Both mother and father feed, protect, and teach the babies for 2 or 3 years.
- ❀ Enemies: Hawks, snakes, tree-climbing cats
- ❀ Home forest: Central and South America

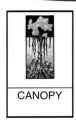

Monkey

When baby monkeys are born, they are strong enough to hold onto their mother's fur. It is not safe for infants to be left alone. Big cats, eagles, wild dogs, snakes, lizards, or other meat-eating animals of the rain forest might kill them. Mothers, older sisters, and aunts watch them closely. These macaques from the Asian rain forest have long tails that make handy leashes for the baby-sitter.

Monkey
(Rhesus Macaque)

* Birthplace: Tree or ground
* Birth weight: 1/2 pound
* Adult weight: 10 to 15 pounds
* Littermates: None
* Favorite food: Babies drink milk; adults eat fruit, insects, seeds, leaves, and small animals.
* Parent care: Mother and the rest of a big family called a *troupe*
* Enemies: Tigers, leopards, big snakes, eagles, wild dogs, lizards
* Home forest: India, China, Vietnam, and islands in Asia

Orangutan

W hat's red, weighs three hundred pounds, and swings in trees? Orangutans! Of course, orangutan babies are not that big. But their fathers are. These big red apes are the largest animals that live in trees. Orangutans rarely come down to the ground. Most of their days are spent eating fruits and leaves at the top of the rain forest canopy.

It rains a lot in rain forests. So it is surprising that an animal that lives there doesn't like to get wet. Orangutans hate it. This two-year-old baby (left) is making an umbrella out of a big leaf.

Orangutan
(Bornean Orangutan)

✿ Birthplace: Tree nest
✿ Birth weight: 3 1/2 pounds
✿ Adult weight: Males, up to 350 pounds; females, about 150 pounds
✿ Littermates: None
✿ Favorite food: Babies drink milk; adults eat fruit, leaves, and insects.
✿ Parent care: Baby stays with mother for 6 or 7 years. Father does not help.
✿ Enemies: In trees, clouded leopards and big snakes; on ground, tigers
✿ Home forest: Asian islands of Borneo and Sumatra

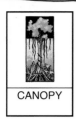

CANOPY

Sloth

The baby sloth likes to take naps. Tip-top naps. In the tallest branches of the rain forest it sleeps away most of the day and all of the night. A snoozing sloth won't fall— even when the wind blows. Long claws wrap around the branches.

Unlike a human baby, the baby sloth never outgrows its need for naps. Even an adult sets aside twenty hours a day for napping. When it's awake, the sloth does everything slowly. It even sneezes in slow motion.

Sloth
(Three-Toed Sloth)

- ❀ Birthplace: Treetop
- ❀ Birth weight: 10 ounces
- ❀ Adult weight: 7 pounds
- ❀ Littermates: None
- ❀ Favorite food: Babies drink milk; adults eat leaves.
- ❀ Parent care: Mother carries baby for 8 months. Father does not help.
- ❀ Enemies: Eagles, hawks, jaguars, snakes
- ❀ Home forest: Central and South America

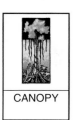

Sugar Glider

The sugar glider jumps out of trees. Without a parachute . . . and at night. Its target is not the ground but a nearby tree. It leaps from tree to tree to get the sweet sap.

Although it looks like a flying squirrel, the sugar glider is not even a close relative. It is a marsupial—an animal with a pouch. Only as big as a mouse, this baby, four weeks out of the pouch, is already a fearless leaper.

Sugar Glider
(Lesser Sugar Glider)

❀ Birthplace: Nest in a hollow tree
❀ Birth weight: Less than a grain of rice
❀ Adult weight: 2 pounds
❀ Littermates: 1
❀ Favorite food: Babies drink only milk for the first 100 days; adults prefer tree sap and gums, insects.
❀ Parent care: Mother keeps babies in pouch for 70 days, then feeds them in nest for another month. Although gliders live in a colony and share a nest, the mother does all the child-raising chores.
❀ Enemies: Quolls, owls, snakes
❀ Home forest: Australia and New Guinea

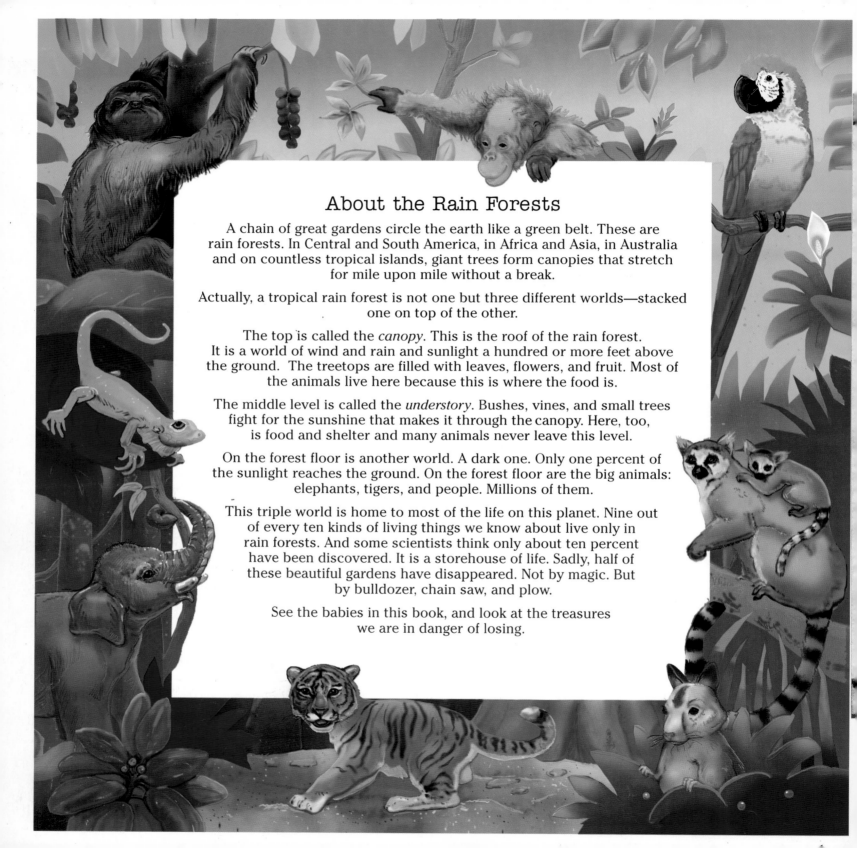

About the Rain Forests

A chain of great gardens circle the earth like a green belt. These are rain forests. In Central and South America, in Africa and Asia, in Australia and on countless tropical islands, giant trees form canopies that stretch for mile upon mile without a break.

Actually, a tropical rain forest is not one but three different worlds—stacked one on top of the other.

The top is called the *canopy*. This is the roof of the rain forest. It is a world of wind and rain and sunlight a hundred or more feet above the ground. The treetops are filled with leaves, flowers, and fruit. Most of the animals live here because this is where the food is.

The middle level is called the *understory*. Bushes, vines, and small trees fight for the sunshine that makes it through the canopy. Here, too, is food and shelter and many animals never leave this level.

On the forest floor is another world. A dark one. Only one percent of the sunlight reaches the ground. On the forest floor are the big animals: elephants, tigers, and people. Millions of them.

This triple world is home to most of the life on this planet. Nine out of every ten kinds of living things we know about live only in rain forests. And some scientists think only about ten percent have been discovered. It is a storehouse of life. Sadly, half of these beautiful gardens have disappeared. Not by magic. But by bulldozer, chain saw, and plow.

See the babies in this book, and look at the treasures we are in danger of losing.